HOW TO
SEEK AND FIND
THE LORD

PETER MASTERS

SWORD & TROWEL
METROPOLITAN TABERNACLE
LONDON

HOW TO SEEK AND FIND THE LORD

© Peter Masters 1993
Booklet edition published in 1994
Eighth printing 2013

SWORD & TROWEL
Metropolitan Tabernacle
Elephant & Castle
London SE1 6SD

ISBN 978 1 890046 02 7

Cover design by Andrew Owen

Printed by Harcourt Litho, Swansea, UK.

How to Seek and Find the Lord

My son, if thou wilt receive my words,
and hide my commandments with thee; so that thou incline
thine ear unto wisdom, and apply thine heart to understanding; yea,
if thou criest after knowledge, and liftest up thy voice for understand-
ing; if thou seekest her as silver, and searchest for her as for hid
treasures; then shalt thou understand the fear of the Lord,
and find the knowledge of God

(*Proverbs 2.1-5; the words of Solomon,*
king of Israel 971-931 BC).

MANY PEOPLE wander far from God, exploring all the attractions of this present world but finding nothing substantial, and much pain and disappointment along the way. Yet, as the years pass, they cling almost desperately to the lifestyle which has failed them. 'If only,' King Solomon seems to say, 'we could put old heads on young shoulders and deliver the next generation from the fraud of a vain world which will steal their minds, hearts and souls, and never keep its promises.'

There is obvious tenderness in the appeal – 'My son, if thou wilt receive my words.' If we would only listen to God and turn to Him we would make great discoveries, receive countless experiences of

His involvement in our lives, and gain wisdom and discernment also. However, there is a small but vital word in the way – 'If ... if ... if'. *If* only we would receive His words, that little word being the condition that decides whether or not we shall find the Lord.

To get the full impact of Solomon's appeal we shall look first at his description of how God has communicated His message to the human race, and then how we must seek Him.

God's message in plain words

'My son, if thou wilt receive *my words*.' These are Solomon's words, but more significantly, they are God's. We notice that Solomon does not speak here of people receiving his *teaching* or *instruction*, but his *words*, and this reminds us that God's message is always expressed in meaningful words.

It is not an unfathomable, mysterious message; a vague, complex thing which you must spend your lifetime trying to figure out. Certainly there are some difficult and deep things in God's revelation, but all the essentials are revealed to us in plain words, such as the facts about God, Who He is, what He is like, His purpose in creating mankind, where mankind has gone wrong, what God has done to save us, and how we may find Him and walk with Him. All these things are expressed in plain, understandable words in the Bible. The fundamental matters which can light up our lives and bring us to God have been revealed by God in a meaningful form of words, and these truths never change.

God's message, then, is not a mystery. We do not draw near to God by spending years in transcendental meditation, or by chasing after strange feelings and mystical insights. Nor is the message of God a form of words which mean one thing to one person and something else to another. It is not strange, religious mumbo-jumbo which cannot be pinned down. King Solomon says, in effect, 'Listen to my words. I am going to teach in plain language, by a series of propositions and understandable statements the truth about God, and how to find Him.'

The Bible is the Book of God in which we are given a logical message about our separation from God, the atonement made for our sins by Jesus Christ, and the availability and nature of conversion. We are told of how Christ the Saviour came from Heaven to suffer the punishment of sin in the place of all who trust in Him for forgiveness, and we are urged to seek Him and to enter into a personal relationship with Him. We are told that if we do so we shall find Him, and that He will change our lives dramatically, bringing us to know Him in this life, and then for ever. These same basic truths are repeated many times through the books of the Bible to confirm our understanding of them.

If we learn nothing else from Solomon's famous appeal, we should learn this – that we cannot find God through the research and study of various religions, but only by listening to *His* revealed Word of explanation about Himself and *His* method of saving souls. It is as we believe and respond to this that we find the Lord. Says Solomon – 'My son, if thou wilt *receive my words.*'

Solomon describes God's message by another term when he tells us to hide His *commandments* within us. Commandments are simply commands, and this term teaches that the message of God is not an option, but something we are bound to obey. God's words carry the force of law for every human soul. If stopped by the police for speeding would we say, 'I'm not surprised, officer, to hear you say that I was going as fast as that, but if you will stand aside I'll just drive on and give some consideration to the matter of what may be a reasonable speed'? This would be a sure way of getting charged!

Remember that we shall eventually be judged for how we react to God's Word. The Lord, in His mercy, speaks persuasively and appealingly, but make no mistake about the fact that He *commands* all people everywhere to repent and to obey. We must never lose sight of the authority of the message because it is expressed with such compassion. There is no alternative to God's method of saving us, and there is no scope for us to work out some original and different way of our own.

Responding leads to conversion

Some of the benefits of being converted are brought out by Solomon's appeal to – 'incline thine ear unto *wisdom*, and apply thine heart to *understanding*.' Do we realise what God is ready to give us? He will give *real* wisdom, that is, skill to handle life. He will give us the capacity to relate to Him, to pray, to understand His Word, and to know His guidance. God is ready to impart these skills to all who listen to His words and respond.

Solomon goes further, describing the experience of finding the Lord in these words: 'Then shalt thou understand the fear of the Lord, and find the knowledge of God.' Here is a great picture of conversion. One moment I am not a believer, having no consciousness of God and no relationship with Him. Then, at conversion, I experience His power in my life and find the eternal and holy God to be full of mercy and kindness. Now, suddenly, I know why Christians stand in awe of Him, and love Him. Now I know why their hearts are completely taken up by Him. I can see it now, because I have seen His kindness for myself, and felt a great change take place in my nature.

Before conversion, God was not there. He was merely a theory, or a possibility. Now after conversion I understand and appreciate His wisdom and power, having been changed in character and desires. That is what it means to be converted – to 'understand the fear of the Lord'.

How, then, can we come to this experience? What does it mean to believe in the Lord, and to find Him? Here we shall look at the *verbs* which Solomon employs to show the way.

1. To believe is to receive God's words

First, Solomon urges us – 'My son, if thou wilt *receive* my words.' *Receive* is the operative word, and the original Hebrew means just that. It means to accept, to embrace, which begins when a person listens with the right attitude, an attitude of respect. You do not listen with suspicion as though to say, 'What's this I'm hearing? I'll give this some thought, but I'm very reluctant to believe it and I intend to question and criticise every part of it, every sentence.' We cannot listen steeped in prejudice or haughty, cynical indifference. The only right way to listen to God is with humble openness. To *receive* means to take something to yourself, value it and possess it. We must come humbly to this Book of God, saying, 'Lord, help me to see its message.'

'This is true,' we must say, 'and a merciful God is offering salvation as a gift. He is teaching me about Himself. Here am I, cut off from God, a sinful rebel, and the mighty God of Heaven is giving me information about Himself and how I may find Him. What will my response be? I'll take it and make it my own. I'll believe it and embrace it.'

This is the only way to come to God's Word. Listen, certainly, with all your reasoning powers, but not in a hostile, critical, unbelieving way, as though God's message is a distasteful thing. Nor in a condescending way, as though you are the superior mind and God is an inferior being. Listen to God as your Maker and Judge, and be receptive, and you will see clearly the words which will lead you to life.

2. *To believe is to make a lifelong commitment*

Solomon's next key verb in telling us how to believe is – '*Hide* my commandments with thee.' The Hebrew word translated *hide* means *hoard,* and while this suggests that we should memorise God's Word, it chiefly means: make it yours for ever. God's salvation changes people for the whole of their remaining lives, and for eternity. Do we realise this is the issue, and this is what we must desire?

When students get down to last-minute, anxious revision they are not primarily interested in how long they will remember the facts they are revising. All that matters is that they remember them for the examination. God's message cannot be received that way. It is no use saying, 'Just at the moment I am going through a troubled phase and I am quite interested in what you have to say. If God could just get me out of my present crisis, it would be enough for me; after that we'll see how things go.' This is not receiving God's message, because God's purpose is to save people for time and eternity, not to help them for a few weeks or months. Believing God's message means I accept that my life will be totally changed by His power, and I desire to become His servant and child throughout life and for ever.

We must say, 'The Bible has lifelong and eternal implications for me. I long to be the Lord's, now and always. This message is not like anything else I learn. This is the salvation of my everlasting soul.' If we come to the Lord in that spirit, God will surely forgive and receive us.

3. To believe is to give undivided attention

Solomon's next verb also conveys an essential aspect of real belief. He says – '*Incline* thine ear unto wisdom.' To *incline* indicates singular concentration. The dog pricks up its ears to hear, and people often tilt their heads to listen. To *incline* the ear is to give careful and undivided attention to one thing only. In this age many influences pressurise us. 'Come with us!' says a godless world, 'Come and join us.' A whole flurry of voices clamour for attention, and in the midst of them is the voice of God in the Bible. But how shall we ever hear this clearly, or believe it, while our attention is drawn to other things? We will never grasp its message, despite its clarity, or feel its urgency while our minds are infatuated with the things of this world, such as the pursuit of selfish ambitions and possessions, and so on.

We will never find the Lord if we listen to Him just once a week, and throughout the rest of it we give our attention to the attractions and temptations of a godless lifestyle. If we say, 'I have so many interests and must first pursue this one and that one,' we will never be converted. 'Single out the voice of God,' says Solomon, 'incline your ear, hang on every word, shut out everything else, and listen for all you're worth.'

You must come to the point when you say, 'I am a lost person, spiritually cut off from God, and this is God's Truth. This message is about life and eternity. This tells me about conversion and the meaning of life. I will listen only to God's message, and give this the highest priority to gain salvation.'

4. To believe is to yield and obey

Is our attitude right as we seek the Lord? Solomon adds another essential piece of counsel when he says: '*Apply* thine heart to understanding.' The Hebrew word translated *apply* means stretch or bend. It is as though the heart is stubborn and inflexible, and it must bend in order to believe, and this is true. By nature we have rebellious and resistant minds, and very fixed opinions to which we cling with great tenacity. We do not easily say, 'All I have ever thought is wrong, and now I will listen to God. This message calls for my response, and I must be ready to give Him my heart and my mind, and to yield myself to Him.'

Believing God's Word is not only a matter of believing that Christ died for sinners to purchase forgiveness and eternal life, essential as all this is, it is about living a new life of obedience to His directions. Solomon therefore calls us to bend and stretch the heart. 'Bend down,' he seems to say, 'surrender yourself, give yourself, and obey the call of God's Word.'

5. To believe is to surrender up pride

Solomon's next appeal shows that real belief is a humble attitude which shows great respect for God. How can we really believe and receive His Word if we have no realisation of His majesty and glory, and no sense of our own smallness and sinfulness before Him? How can we believe a message warning of judgement and hell without feeling the *urgency* of our lost condition? Solomon puts it this way: 'Yea, if thou *criest* after knowledge'.

In the *Book of Proverbs* King Solomon wrote many miniature parables, and these words picture a child who cries out for something from a parent. They illustrate an inferior person appealing for something from a superior; a junior asking something of a senior. The needy inferior cries out for the thing which he urgently needs. A child wants something which he cannot get for himself, so he must plead with the one who can provide it. This is the way in which Almighty God must be approached by sinful men and women seeking forgiveness and conversion.

We cannot secure by anything we can do the forgiveness of our sins. Nor can we produce spiritual life for ourselves, so that we may relate to God. We cannot even understand the message of salvation without God's help. We are poor, lost sinners needing the Saviour, and to believe is to feel these needs, and to see that only Christ can meet them. Therefore we *cry* out to God acknowledging our sinfulness and helplessness, and trusting only in the amazing act of Christ, the Second Person of the one eternal Godhead, Who came to earth as our sinbearer to atone for sinners.

Proud, self-sufficient, self-confident people cannot *cry* to God. They may try, but their prayers will have a hollow ring, because they say, almost reluctantly and with no sense of their guilt and danger, 'O God, if You are there, show Yourself to me.' This is not true prayer, and God will not answer it. The person who believes the message of God's Word cries out in the manner of one who is in great need, and really depends upon what the Saviour has done as he asks for forgiveness and new life.

6. To believe is to grasp our distance from God

Solomon then extends his illustration to show yet another aspect of rightly approaching the Lord. He speaks of our needing to 'lift up' our voice for understanding. This is no longer the picture of a child calling across the room to its parent, but of someone far away who must shout at the top of his voice to be heard. Perhaps a child has dashed across the fields and become suddenly alarmed at the distance between him and his parents. Or perhaps a trader is passing at a distance and needs to be hailed.

Lifting up the voice suggests distance, and this is another factor in our hopeless spiritual condition which must alarm us as we seek the

Lord. If unconverted, we are far from God, having no interaction with Him, no help, no guidance, in fact nothing. We live merely as material creatures, under the condemnation of the God Who made us and Whose authority and kindness we have spurned.

We must recognise that we are separated from God by a vast chasm of guilt, and that we are in eternal danger. This is the attitude of authentic prayer which will bring us to God. We do not come saying, 'I am quite a decent person, Lord, but I need a little bit of grace: so help me in my life.' We come as sinners who are a long way from Him, and we plead for Him to draw us near, and give us new life and a close relationship with Him. Solomon illustrates the earnestness we need in terms of an urgent, loud shout.

7. To believe is to desire conversion

Still further help from Solomon comes in his words – 'If thou *seekest* her [spiritual wisdom and knowledge] as silver.' The Hebrew word translated *seek* means simply to look for something which you do not possess, or have mislaid. But here, the search is particularly vigorous because something of great value is sought, namely, *silver,* which refers to crafted ornaments of great beauty and value. The picture is of a merchant seeking out the best articles from craftsmen in many cities. It is his livelihood, and the prosperity and survival of his family depends on his success. He has an eye for what is good, and is drawn to the places where the best *objets d'art* are found.

The application of the picture is this: God's salvation (forgiveness, new life and a walk with the Lord) is like valuable silver to the ancient merchant, objects of incalculable value and unsurpassed in beauty. How much, therefore, must we desire these things as we visit the sources of them, such as God's Word, and churches where the way of salvation is explained.

As the seeker after silver spared no effort to secure his prize, so we must not rest until the treasure of salvation is ours. We will go to God in prayer, longing for the definite experience of His touch upon our life. We must tell the merciful God that our life is nothing without Christ and the new beginning which He alone can give, and that we will value this as the highest gift in the universe. What could be more precious than to be certain that our sins are forgiven and that Christ, the Redeemer and the only Mediator between God and man, is our Saviour. This, says Solomon, is the heartfelt attitude of the person who sincerely seeks the Lord – He is beyond price!

8. To believe is to be a persistent seeker

The final word of help from Solomon on the right way of seeking salvation warns about the impediments and dangers to seekers, and tells how these must be handled. Solomon says: 'If thou seekest her as silver, and *searchest* for her as for hid treasures; then shalt thou understand.'

The Hebrew word *seek*, as we saw, refers to looking for something which is hard to find, but the word *search* speaks of something very deeply hidden or concealed. This word refers to mining. It is about excavating the rock to find precious metals and gemstones. Mining was hard and dirty work in Bible times, and this picture is very apt for the hardships and also the great rewards of seeking the Lord.

Mining illustrates well our search for blessings which at the time of our seeking are *unseen*, being hidden in the rock. We begin to pray to God, saying, 'O, Lord, I repent of my sin; reveal Thyself to me and make me one of Thy children. Lord, change me and give me spiritual life.' But at the time we pray the blessing is still unknown to us. In a sense we pray in darkness because we have no personal experience of God's love and power, and have not yet felt His nearness.

We say, 'I am not there yet, Lord. I have not yet felt Thy hand on my life. I am shut out. O, Lord, I recognise I am a lost sinner, excluded from Heaven, unconverted and far from Thee. Lord, may I find Thee, discover Thee, know Thee and hold on to Thee.'

How like mining for precious stones this is! The miner longs to discover the precious things, and although as seekers we can do nothing to contribute to the securing of forgiveness, yet there is a hard part to seeking. Imagine the painful toil in mining before the days of explosives. Imagine the jarred limbs and grazed knuckles, and the days of patient tunnelling. Imagine also the strong temptation to leave the mine and escape to the fresh air.

It is the same with seeking the Lord. As the seeker sets off for church or opens a Bible, the tempter begins the process of drawing the heart and mind to other things. 'Watch television; do this or that. Do anything but seek the Lord.' But the seeker must push these distractions aside and press on to hear God's Word and pray for salvation. As a seeker you must never forget the antagonism of our spiritual enemy the devil, and you must be determined not to be put off.

Mining also involved danger and fear, because shafts collapsed, rocks fell, and flooding occurred. Similarly, the person who seeks the Lord often encounters dangers and pains such as the scorn of friends, or the surrender of sinful habits to which he has become very deeply attached. Many have left off seeking the Lord because of fear of these difficulties, but just as the old-time miner was more afraid of destitution and starvation than the dangers of the mine, so the person who believes God's Word must be more concerned about the pointlessness of a godless life, the death of the soul, and a lost eternity, than about the scorn of friends, and other hazards.

Mining (in Bible times) pictures a further difficulty for those who seek the Lord, because it was full of doubts and demoralising influences. In an age when it took so many weeks to drive a tunnel a mere ten or twenty feet into the rock, the sponsor of the mine suffered many anxious hours wondering whether anything of value would be found. Would the blood, sweat, toil and cost be worth it? Would they at last strike gold or silver?

When we seek the Lord, the devil aims to distract and demoralise us with constant doubts. We are tempted to doubt the existence of God, the character of God, and the message of God. If we persist in our seeking, we may even be tempted to doubt our own sincerity. But the person who seeks the Lord must fix his trust upon the promises of God, and believe that he will find God through repentance and faith. He must sweep aside all these doubts.

Mining illustrates how we should seek the Lord in yet another important respect. Mining, after all, is the process of removing unwanted soil, dirt and rock, in order to get something precious, and the procedure for seeking and finding the Lord is just the same. It involves repenting of my sin and trusting in what Christ has done on Calvary to take away my filthy guilt. It is crying out to God to take away my wilful, unfeeling, selfish, unconverted heart, and to give me a new one. There can be no discovery of God until Christ removes the guilt and dross of sin. The priceless treasure of salvation cannot be found without sincere repentance.

Finally, the mining picture, though showing the harder side of seeking, shows also the mighty *grace* of God. Hard as mining was in Bible times, it could bring to the miners a fortune to last a lifetime. A farmer may labour all his life and only meet the basic needs of his family, but a miner who struck gold would never need to work again. In three months he might take himself into a world of lasting wealth and luxury. Yet the miner did not *make* the gold or silver or precious stones which he found. He neither invented nor designed his discoveries, nor did he fashion them into articles of beauty. Nevertheless, he received more than anyone else involved in any known trade of those days. To him came 'discovered' treasure.

What a picture this is of what happens when we believe God's Word and seek Him! All we do is believe, repent and ask for salvation, and what is there to that? My 'toil' is really nothing at all compared with the incalculable value of salvation. The Saviour pays for my salvation entirely, having suffered in my place, for my sin, and having offered up His own perfect righteousness to earn eternal blessing for me. I deserve nothing, but I receive everything – pardon, new life, adoption into the family of God, and eternal treasure. A condemned and guilty sinner, I gain by the gift of God the everlasting salvation of my soul. The 'grace' of God (His unmerited and unearned favour to me) is my only hope and trust.

If this is the manner in which we seek the Lord, 'then,' says

Solomon, 'shalt thou understand the fear of the Lord, and find the knowledge of God.' He *will* hear our cry, and He will wash away our sin, and bring us to a conscious knowledge that we belong to Him, and that He has saved us. Do not leave out any of the vital elements of a seeking prayer, as you repent of sin, state your entire trust in the work of Christ Jesus the Saviour, and yield your life entirely to Him for ever.

My son,
if thou wilt receive my words,
and hide my commandments with thee;
so that thou incline thine ear unto wisdom, and
apply thine heart to understanding; yea, if thou criest
after knowledge, and liftest up thy voice for understanding;
if thou seekest her as silver, and searchest for her as
for hid treasures; then shalt thou understand
the fear of the Lord, and find the
knowledge of God
(Proverbs 2.1-5).

Other publications by Dr Masters, helpful to those seeking the Lord or new to the Christian life, are listed overleaf.

Other booklets by Dr Masters:

Vanity of Vanities

Subtitled *The Emptiness of Life Without God*. Presents the experience of King Solomon, who experimented with every conceivable kind of pleasure, and concluded that life is pointless and predictable, unless people seek and find the Lord God, and know His power and guidance in their lives.

The Rebellious Years

Subtitled *The Need for Self-Understanding*, this booklet is intended to help readers from mid-teenage to late twenties to understand the source of the inner rebellion that urges us all away from God in the 'second quarter' of life.

What You Should Know About Your Conscience

What is the mysterious faculty of conscience, and how does it function? What happens when it is abused, or attempts are made to reprogramme it? Can it cause psychosomatic illness? Here are all the vital facts clearly demonstrated with case histories. Here too, is the only effective way of unburdening or 'purging' the hurting conscience.

A Seeker's Problems

This booklet answers ten problems encountered by serious seekers. These are not questions or doubts about the faith, but personal hindrances in approaching Christ, by faith. Many seekers have been helped by the advice given here.

Available from: Tabernacle Bookshop, Metropolitan Tabernacle, Elephant & Castle, London SE1 6SD   www.TabernacleBookshop.org

**Audio and video sermons of Dr Masters
are available free on the Metropolitan Tabernacle's website:
www.MetropolitanTabernacle.org**